Memories of Aleppo

Our Favorite Middle Eastern Recipes

Seta Ekmekji & Rhoda Margossian

Photography by Raffi Alexander Ekmekji
Cover Design by Margaux Alexander

• • •

First Edition July 2016
Published by Spiderbox Photography

Spiderbox™

Forward

Aleppo is a city in Northern Syria that dates back to 4000 B.C. Its population is diverse, comprised of a majority of Arabs alongside numerous other ethnicities such as Armenians, Jews, Assyrians and Greeks. These cultures, and the domination of the region by the Ottomans, have contributed to the cuisine of Aleppo. It is the only city besides Paris to have been awarded the Grand Prize of the International Gastronomic Academy.

We, Rhoda and Seta, are two Armenian women born and raised in Aleppo between 1930 and 1965. We were schoolmates in the American High School for Girls. Later on one of us married the other's brother and we became relatives as well as very close friends, and still we are close today in spite of all the quibbling we experienced writing this book.

These recipes represent some of the foods we ate growing up in Aleppo. The recipes we included in this book are the ones that our families loved the most, and some of them have the power to transport us back in time. I, Rhoda, remember once when I was baking the dessert Karabij, here at my home in California when my son came home from school and exclaimed "Oh, the house smells like Aleppo".

Many of the recipes in this book are for dishes that are healthy and delicious, both vegetarian and vegan. Much of this cuisine is based on vegetables, grains, legumes, and fruits. Olive oil is the predominant lipid and fresh lemon juice is the primary source of acidity. In addition, many dishes call for yogurt.

We hope this book adds to your eating pleasures.

Rhoda & Seta

To our readers,
To succeed with these recipes
use common sense and your taste buds.
Love,
Seta and Rhoda

Aleppo pepper is a fundamental spice used in Middle Eastern cuisine. It is commonly found in Middle Eastern grocery stores. You may substitute Aleppo pepper with crushed Korean red pepper widely available in Korean supermarkets.

Contents

Soups

SOUPS

Ades Hamod (Sour Lentil Soup with Swiss Chard) 8

Yogurt Soup with Rice 8

Spinach Soup with Tahini 10

Tanabour (Cold Yogurt Soup with Hulled Barley) 11

Makhlouta or Vartabed Soup (Red Split Lentil Soup) 12

• ● •

ADES HAMOD
Lentil Soup with Swiss Chard and Lemon Juice

1 cup whole lentils, green or brown
¼ cup split red lentils
6 cups water
¼ cup bulgur #1
1 bunch Swiss chard, cleaned and chopped
⅓ cup extra virgin olive oil
3 cloves garlic, crushed
1 Tablespoon dry mint, crushed
5 Tablespoons lemon juice
1 teaspoon Aleppo red pepper
Salt to taste

1. Rinse lentils and place in a pot with the water. Add the bulgur and bring to a boil.

2. Wash and coarsely chop the Swiss chard and add to the pot.

3. Add olive oil, lemon juice, mint, salt and red pepper, and bring back to a boil. Simmer covered for 45 minutes until well cooked.

Serve hot or warm.

YOGURT SOUP WITH RICE

This yogurt based soup has a soothing and comforting effect, specially for an upset stomach. Seta's brother Dr. Shahnour Adrian used to prescribe this soup to his patients. It is also delicious comfort food.

⅓ cup rice
3 cups water
2 cups yogurt
1 egg
3 Tablespoons butter
1 Tablespoon dried mint
½ tsp salt to taste

1. In a pot boil 3 cups water. Add the rinsed rice and cook for about half an hour, until rice is soft and creamy

2. Put the yogurt in a bowl and whisk in an egg. Ladle in a few spoons of the cooked rice from the pot and stir to tamper yogurt. Pour the yogurt mixture into the pot and mix well.

3. Melt the butter in a pan until it browns a little and mix in the dried mint and stir. Poor it over the soup in the pot.

SPINACH SOUP WITH TAHINI PASTE

7 cups water
¼ cup bulgur #1
½ cup onions, chopped
1 pound spinach, cleaned and coarsely chopped or one lb frozen chopped spinach
1½ teaspoons salt
¼ teaspoon black pepper
¾ cup tahini

Garnish to taste: freshly squeezed lemon juice and Aleppo red pepper

1. Put water, onion and bulgur in a pot and bring to a boil. Reduce heat and simmer for 10 minutes until tender. Add the spinach and salt, cook for 5 more minutes, and add black pepper. Remove from heat.

2. Make the tahini sauce in a bowl by blending together tahini and one cup of the soup broth. Slowly pour back the tahini mixture into the pot, stirring constantly. Reheat the soup.

3. Serve with lemon juice and Aleppo red pepper according to your taste.

TAHNABOUR
Cold Yogurt Soup with Hulled Barley

1 cup hulled barley
5 cups water
1 teaspoon salt
3 cups yogurt

1. In a bowl, soak barley about 8 hours (or overnight) in 3 cups water. Transfer barley and soaking water to a pot, add 2 more cups of water and bring to a boil. Simmer covered for 1½ hours or until barley is tender and most of the water is absorbed. Add salt. Let cool.

2. Beat the yogurt into a smooth paste. Gradually add the yogurt into the cooked and cooled barley. Serve cold.

MAKHLOUTA OR VARTABED SOUP
Red Split Lentil Soup

Makhlouta is the quintessential comfort food, well suited for cold nights. Increasing the amount of Aleppo pepper will work wonders to both body and soul.

1½ cup split red lentil
¼ cup rice (medium grain)
1 large yellow onion, chopped
6 cups water
¼ cup bulgur #1 or ¼ cup pearl barley
⅓ cup olive oil
1 red bell pepper, coarsely chopped
2 teaspoons cumin powder

Toppings:
2 Tablespoons yellow onion, minced
2 Tablespoons olive oil
1 pita bread, cut into two inch triangles
1 pinch Aleppo red pepper

1. Rinse the lentils and rice and place in a pot with the onions and water. Add bulgur, olive oil, red bell pepper and cumin and bring to a boil. Reduce heat, cover and simmer. Cook until creamy, about 1½ hours, stirring often. Add water if it becomes too thick.

2. For the topping, fry minced onion in olive oil. Toast pita triangles until they are light brown and crispy. Garnish each serving of the soup with the onions, pita bread, and sprinkle with Aleppo red pepper.

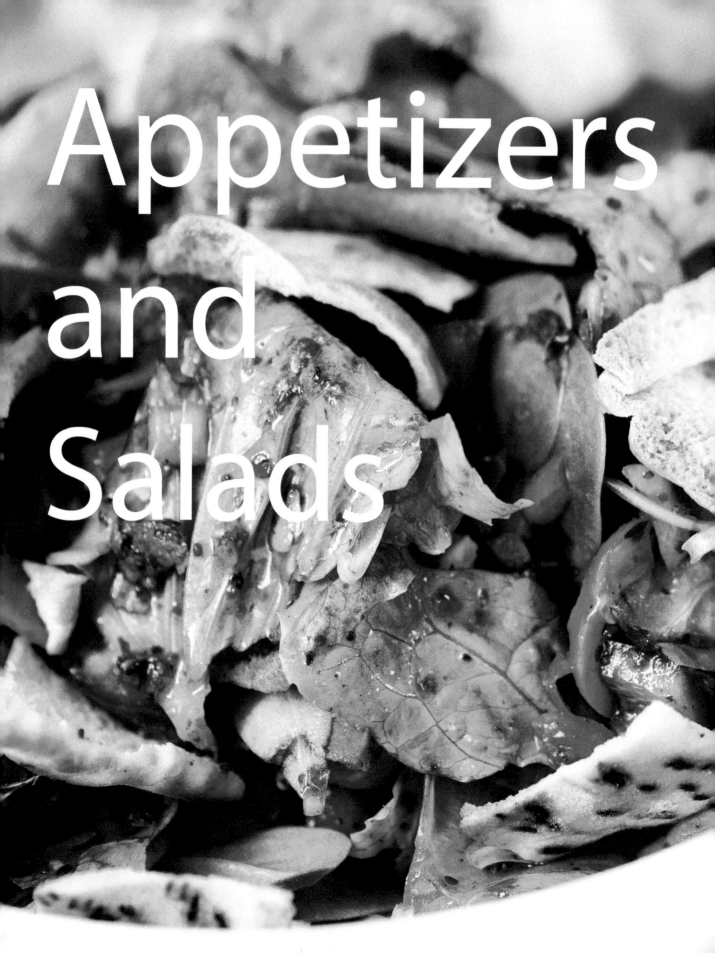

Appetizers
and
Salads

APPETIZERS AND SALADS

• • •

AJJEH
Vegetable Omelet

This is a dish that is commonly made during Easter. It is prepared traditionally using a special frying pan sold in Middle Eastern stores. You may substitute using a cast iron muffin pan.

5 eggs
1 Tablespoon all purpose flour
1 bunch parsley, minced
1 small yellow onion, minced
4 stalks green onion, chopped
2 cloves garlic, minced
½ bunch fresh mint, minced (or 1½ teaspoon dry mint)
¼ teaspoon black pepper
¼ teaspoon allspice
¼ teaspoon cinnamon
1 teaspoon Aleppo red pepper
1 teaspoon salt to taste
½ teaspoon baking soda
olive oil for frying

1. In a large bowl, break the eggs and beat lightly. Add all the remaining ingredients and mix lightly.

2. Heat the pan. If using a pan with indentations (rounded cavities), add olive oil into each indentation. When hot, drop in one heaping Tablespoon of the mixture. Turn the heat to medium and cook for approximately 3 minutes on each side. Remove and place on paper towels to drain excess oil.

Note:
If using a regular, non-stick frying pan, add oil to the pan and when hot, pour one heaping Tablespoon of the egg mixture on the pan several times, leaving some space between each pour (you may have to use a spatula to keep the various pours of egg mixture apart from each other). Turn the heat to medium and cook 3 minutes on each side.

ARMENIAN SALAD

1 large tomato, cubed ½ inch
4 small cucumbers, diced ¼ inch
1 medium onion or 4 green onions, finely chopped
2 jalapeño peppers or ½ bell pepper, finely chopped
1 bunch parsley, finely chopped
1 bunch fresh mint, finely chopped (or 1 Tablespoon dried crushed mint)
½ teaspoon salt to taste
1 teaspoon Aleppo red pepper
1 clove garlic, crushed
¼ cup lemon juice (or less, to taste)
2 teaspoons tomato paste
¼ cup extra virgin olive oil

Mix all the ingredients and adjust seasonings to taste.

BABA GHANOUJ OR MOUTABBAL
Eggplant Dip

Baba Ghanouj is a dip with unique flavors. In Arabic, the name means pampered father, which gives a hint about its special place on a menu. Every country in the Middle East has its own version of this dish. The main ingredient in baba ghanouj is of course, the eggplant. The version in this cookbook uses yogurt instead of tomatoes, which imparts softer subtler taste. Like hoummus, it is a dip that can be eaten with pita bread.

1 large eggplant
1 ½ Tablespoons tahini
1 Tablespoon yogurt
1 clove garlic, minced
1 Tablespoon lemon juice (or more, to taste)
salt to taste

Garnish:
2 Tablespoons parsley, chopped
½ teaspoon Aleppo red pepper
extra virgin olive oil
2 Tablespoons pomegranate seeds, optional

1 to 2 pita breads, warmed

1. Prick the eggplant in several places with a fork. Broil or grill (ideally on mesquite charcoal) until the eggplant is soft and charred. Let cool.

2. Cut the eggplant in half (lengthwise) and scoop out the inside, discarding as many of the seeds as possible. Chop the eggplant, then mash it with a fork (never in a blender or food processor).

3. In a separate bowl combine the tahini, yogurt, minced garlic, lemon juice and salt. Mix well and stir into the mashed eggplant.

4. To serve, spread on a plate and sprinkle with chopped parsley and Aleppo red pepper, drizzle with olive oil.

5. Sprinkle pomegranate seeds when in season.

6. Serve with warm pita bread.

Note: The best way to eat Baba Ghanouj is to scoop it up with a piece of pita bread the same way as one would eat guacamole using chips.

BEUREG
Fillo Dough Stuffed with Cheese

Although this recipe is made with cheese, there are several types of beuregs, made either with spinach, or with meat and pine nuts. No matter which version is served, they make an excellent finger food.

1 package fillo dough
½ cup (1 stick) unsalted butter, melted
½ cup vegetable oil

Filling:
10 oz white cheese. El Cacique Queso Blanco, shredded
(from Middle Eastern stores)
1 egg
2 Tablespoons parsley, chopped
2 Tablespoons dill, chopped (or 1 teaspoon dried dill)
salt and white pepper to taste

Egg wash: (optional)
1 egg, beaten
1 teaspoon water

Preheat oven to 350 degrees F

1. Mix melted butter and vegetable oil in a bowl. Set aside.

2. Cut the stack of fillo dough into 2 square-shaped stacks. Cover one stack and place in the refrigerator.

3. From the first stack, take two fillo sheets and brush the top sheet with the melted butter mixture. Place 1 teaspoon cheese filling in the middle of the sheet, fold ⅓ of the sheet (from one edge) over the middle third of the sheet (that has the cheese) and brush with the melted butter. Then fold the last 3rd of the sheet onto the part you just brushed with butter. Brush the top sheet with butter. Start folding like the American flag giving it a triangular shape. Repeat with remaining sheets.

4. Repeat step 3 using the second stack of dough (that you placed in the fridge). This process yields about 25 small beuregs.

5. Place beuregs on a baking tray and freeze for 2 hours. Remove from freezer. Brush with egg wash and bake beuregs in a preheated 350 F degree oven for 20 minutes or until golden brown.

Note: Unbaked beuregs can keep for several months in the freezer if kept in a tight container. Do not thaw them before baking.

EECH
Bulgur Salad

½ cup onion, finely chopped
½ cup olive oil
1½ cups tomatoes, finely chopped (or 16 oz canned tomato)
2 Tablespoons tomato paste
1 teaspoon Aleppo red pepper
1 teaspoon salt
3 Tablespoons lemon juice (or more, to taste)
1 cup bulgur #1
¾ cup water

12-14 romaine lettuce leaves, cleaned and separated

1. Sauté chopped onions in olive oil until translucent. Add the tomato paste and mix. Add the tomatoes, salt, Aleppo red pepper, lemon juice, water and bring to a boil.

2. Add the bulgur, mix well, cover and remove from the stove top.

3. Let stand for half an hour, then using a fork, fluff the bulgur mix, adding some water if it is too dry. Portion ¼ cup of the bulgur salad into each lettuce leaf. Arrange on a platter and serve. This may also be served as a mound in the center of a plate with lettuce leaves arranged in a circle around it.

Note: can be prepared and refrigerated one day in advance.

FRIED EGGPLANT

1 large eggplant
½ teaspoon salt
2 eggs, lightly beaten
¼ teaspoon salt
¼ teaspoon black pepper
2 Tablespoons all purpose flour
¼ cup extra virgin olive oil

1. Cut the stems off the eggplants. Peel off three lengthwise strips of the eggplant skin and discard. Cut the eggplant lengthwise or crosswise into ½ inch wide slices. Sprinkle eggplant slices with salt and let sit for 2 hours Squeeze the eggplant slices between paper towels to remove excess liquid.

2. In a frying pan, heat the olive oil on medium and take care not to burn the oil.

3. Beat the eggs and add the salt and pepper. Dip the eggplant slices in the flour and then in the beaten egg.

4. Fry eggplant on both sides until golden brown.

EKMEK ASHI
Sour and Spicy Pita Bread Stew

Ekmek Ashi is essentially a poor man's stew because it uses day-old bread instead of meat. But poor men know how to eat, often even better than rich men. In this dish, the flavors of tomato, garlic, red pepper, and olive oil virtually dance around the day-old bread and bring it to life. It's Nicole's favorite.

1 Tablespoon sumac powder
½ cup water
¼ cup extra virgin olive oil
10 cloves peeled garlic, whole
1 15 ounce can chopped tomatoes
1 Tablespoon tomato paste
1 teaspoon Aleppo red pepper
1 teaspoon salt
1 red bell pepper , cut into chunks
2 Tablespoons lemon juice
3 old pita breads torn into pieces (1 to 2 inches wide)

1. Make sumac water by boiling the sumac powder in ½ cup of water for a few minutes. Strain the liquid, discarding the sumac pulp.

2. In a frying pan, heat the olive oil. Add the garlic and lightly sauté. Add the remaining ingredients to the garlic except the bread. Bring the mixture to a boil, taste and adjust seasonings. Add the bread chunks, turn off heat and cover pan.

3. Wait for 15 minutes, then fluff the mixture with a fork and serve on a platter.

FATTOUSH
Lebanese Salad with Pita Croutons

Dressing:
1 clove garlic, crushed
½ cup extra virgin olive oil
4 stalks green onions, finely chopped
¼ red bell pepper, thinly sliced
1 medium radish, thinly sliced
zest of 1 lemon
1 Tablespoon dry mint, crushed
¼ teaspoon black pepper, crushed
1 teaspoon salt
1 teaspoon Aleppo red pepper
2 Tablespoons sumac powder
½ cup lemon juice

Salad:
2 medium-sized tomatoes, diced
½ cup minced fresh mint
1 cup cucumbers, diced
1 cup parsley, minced
½ bell pepper, thinly sliced
2 bunches purslane (if not available use watercress)
½ head romaine lettuce

1. In a small bowl, make the dressing by combining all the dressing ingredients. Set aside.

2. Separate 2 pita breads into 4 halves and toast in oven until light brown. Break into bite size pieces and set aside.

3. In a large mixing bowl, gently toss all salad ingredients. Pour the dressing over the salad and mix well. Add the toasted bread just before serving and toss gently. Adjust the seasoning. Fattoush should have a sour taste.

FOUL [fool]
Fava Bean Salad

Fool is the classic and ancient Middle Eastern breakfast, going back to Egypt of the 5th century BC. It is also mentioned in the Talmud Yerushalmi, *indicating that it was used in Middle Eastern countries since the fourth century. In every Middle Eastern city you'll find restaurants that serve nothing but this dish, either for eat-in or take-out.*

1 15 ounce can fava beans
(drained and rinsed)

¼ cup water
1 clove garlic, crushed
1 teaspoon cumin powder
1 teaspoon Aleppo red pepper
salt to taste
2 Tablespoons fresh lemon juice

1 medium tomato, chopped finely
1 Tablespoon parsley, chopped
¼ cup extra virgin olive oil

½ white onion, sliced lengthwise into wedges
8 sprigs of fresh mint
pita bread

1. In a medium sized pot, add the fava beans. Add a quarter cup water and bring to a boil. Simmer uncovered for five minutes. Remove from stove top.

2. Add the garlic, cumin, Aleppo red pepper, salt and lemon juice. Adjust the seasoning with salt and lemon juice. At this point the fava beans should taste sour.

3. To serve, place a serving of fava beans in a bowl, top it off with some of the tomatoes and their liquid, as well as parsley and olive oil.

4. Serve with pita bread, onion and fresh mint. The best way to eat fool is to scoop fava beans (and tomatoes) up with a piece of pita bread.

Note: Chop extra tomatoes because, invariably, you will want to add more tomatoes to the bowl of fool.

GREEN BEANS WITH TOMATO SAUCE

A simple but exquisite vegetarian dish that can be served cold or at room temperature. Just use a piece of pita bread to scoop up the delicious goodness.

1 lb green beans
½ cup extra virgin olive oil
1 jalapeño pepper, thinly sliced
8 cloves garlic, sliced
1 cup tomato sauce
1 tsp salt to taste
1 Tablespoon sugar
2 Tablespoons red wine vinegar

1. Wash the beans, trim off the ends of the beans, put in a pot and cover with water. Bring it to a boil and cook until the beans are tender, about 25 minutes. Drain and set beans aside.

2. Heat a sauté pan, add a third of the olive oil. When oil is hot add the jalapeño pepper and stir. Add the garlic, stir while cooking so garlic does not burn, for about 1 minute. Add the tomato sauce, salt, sugar and vinegar and stir. Add the beans and cook for 10 minutes on medium heat uncovered.

3. Adjust seasoning (salt, sugar, vinegar).

4. When cool, stir in remaining olive oil.

HOUMMOS
Garbanzo Bean Dip

1 15 ounce can garbanzo beans, (drained and rinsed)
4 Tablespoons lemon juice
1 teaspoon cumin
1 clove garlic, crushed
4 Tablespoons extra virgin olive oil
¼ teaspoon salt
2 Tablespoons tahini paste
Aleppo red pepper
1 Tablespoon parsley, chopped
pita bread

1. Put the beans in food processor and add lemon juice, cumin, garlic, 2 tablespoons olive oil and salt. Process until it becomes a smooth paste. If thick, add some water. Add tahini and process again until very smooth. It should have the consistency of tomato paste. Adjust seasoning.

2. To serve, spread in a dish and sprinkle with cumin powder, Aleppo red pepper, chopped parsley, and drizzle with 2 tablespoons of olive oil.

3. Serve with warmed pita bread.

IMAM BAYILDI
Eggplant, Tomato & Pepper Ragout

6 small Japanese or Italian eggplants
6 cloves peeled garlic, whole
¼ cup green bell pepper, coarsely chopped
¼ cup red bell pepper, coarsely chopped
5 Roma tomatoes, ¼ inch slices
6 sprigs of parsley
6 Tablespoons extra virgin olive oil
¼ cup tomato sauce
¼ cup water
1 teaspoon salt
¼ teaspoon black pepper
1 teaspoon crushed red pepper

1. Cut the stems off the eggplants. Peel off three lengthwise strips of the eggplant skin.

2. Along each of the peeled strips of the eggplant, create a pocket by slitting an inch lengthwise through the eggplant.Stuff the pockets with garlic, red and green pepper chunks, and sliced tomatoes. Tie each eggplant with the parsley sprig.

3. Arrange eggplants tightly in a saucepan. Drizzle 1 tablespoon of olive oil on each eggplant.

4. Mix tomato sauce and ¼ cup water, salt, black pepper and Aleppo red pepper. Pour over the eggplants. Cover and simmer for half an hour or until the eggplants are tender. Let cool in the pan.

5. Arrange on a serving platter and serve at room temperature.

JAJEK WITH SWISS CHARD
Yogurt Salad (A Traditional Easter Dish)

2 bunches Swiss chard, coarsely
chopped
1 cup water
1 cup parsley, finely chopped
1 clove garlic, crushed
1 teaspoon salt
½ cup fresh mint, finely chopped
2 cups labneh (strained yogurt)
½ cup green onions, finely chopped

1. Wash and coarsely chop the Swiss chard, place in a pot and add one cup of water. Bring to a boil, then simmer for 10 minutes, drain in a colander and let cool. Squeeze the liquid out of the Swiss chard and put in a bowl.

2. Mix the Swiss chard with the parsley, crushed garlic, salt, fresh mint and labneh. This mix should be thick. Adjust for salt. Spread the labneh mixture on a platter and lightly coat it with additional plain labneh to give it a white color. Garnish with chopped green onions and additional parsley.

JAJEK WITH CUCUMBERS
Yogurt Salad

1½ cups peeled and diced cucumbers
½ teaspoon salt
2 cups yogurt
2 teaspoons crushed dry mint
1 clove garlic, crushed

1. In a bowl, sprinkle salt on the cucumbers and toss.

2. In another bowl, mix yogurt, crushed dry mint, and crushed garlic. Add the yogurt mixture to the cucumbers and mix, then refrigerate until serving time.

KHEBZEH JEBNEH MSAASAA
Grilled Cheese Sandwich

1 pita bread
¼ inch slices of El Cacique Queso Fresco (available in Mexican and Armenian markets) or other similar white cheese
½ teaspoon Aleppo red pepper
½ teaspoon crushed dry mint
1 Tablespoon extra virgin olive oil

Preheat oven to 350 degrees F

1. Open the pita bread so you have 2 disks. Place the sliced cheese onto one of the pita disks. Sprinkle red pepper, mint and drizzle with olive oil. Then cover with the remaining pita disk.

2. Place the pita directly on center rack of 350 F oven and toast for 5 minutes or until lightly brown and crisp.

3. Put the toasted pita between two pieces of paper towels or brown paper bag and press with the palm of your hands. Cut into quarters and serve.

MUHAMMARA
Red Pepper and Walnut Dip

Muhammara is yet another delicacy of contrasting flavors: red pepper, pomegranate molasses, and walnuts. Its magical qualities lie in the fact that when you eat it, you can taste all of these wonderful flavors simultaneously. Although muhammara is usually eaten as a dip, it goes very well with turkey, especially left-over turkey. Muhammara and turkey between two slices of toasted bread makes a perfect sandwich.

6 red bell peppers, coarsely chopped and seeded
½ cup corn flake crumbs
1 teaspoon cumin powder
½ teaspoon salt (or to taste)
2 teaspoons Aleppo red pepper (or more depending how spicy you like it)
1 Tablespoon granulated sugar
3 Tablespoons lemon juice
2 Tablespoons pomegranate syrup
1 Tablespoon red pepper paste (optional) found in Middle Eastern stores
½ cup extra virgin olive oil
1 cup walnuts, chopped (pulse 10 times in the food processor)
pine nuts for garnish

1. In a food processor, add chopped bell peppers and process until smooth. Put in a saucepan and bring to a boil. Cook uncovered for 10 minutes. (Six bell peppers will make 1 cup of pepper sauce). Remove from stove top and cool.

2. Mix red pepper sauce with the corn flake crumbs (don't use bread crumbs). Add the cumin powder, salt, Aleppo red pepper, granulated sugar, lemon juice, pomegranate syrup and optional red pepper paste. Mix well. Then add olive oil and chopped walnuts. Sauce should taste sweet, hot and sour. If it is thick, add some water gradually until it has the consistency of a dip. Serve on a plate and decorate with pine nuts.

MOUJADDARA
Lentil and Rice Pilaf

Moujaddara is a dish found in almost every Middle Eastern home. It's also a classic example of a dish that's greater than the sum of its parts. There are many recipes for Moujaddara and each country, each town or city has its own version. To experience it fully, try it with pickles (cucumber or jalapeño) and with a salad of tomatoes, cucumbers, and scallions dressed with lemon juice and olive oil.

1 cup green or brown lentils
3 cups water
½ cup Basmati rice
¼ teaspoon salt
⅓ cup extra virgin olive oil
1 medium yellow onion, thinly sliced lengthwise
¼ teaspoon black pepper

1. Rinse lentils in cold water and drain. Place lentils and 3 cups of water in a pot and bring to a boil, then simmer covered for 10 minutes.

2. Rinse rice and add to the lentils in the pot and bring to a boil, add salt and simmer covered on a very low heat for about 30 minutes until all the water is absorbed, and both lentils and rice are cooked. If they are still not cooked, add a few tablespoons of water and cook a little longer.

3. While the lentils and rice are cooking, heat the olive oil in a frying pan, add the onions and fry on medium low heat, stirring frequently until onions turn golden brown, about 10 minutes. Remove the onions with a slotted spoon and put aside.

4. Pour the hot olive oil (in which the onions were cooked) over the lentil and rice. Let rest for 5 to 10 minutes, then fluff with a fork. Place the Moujaddara on a serving plate and garnish with the crisp onions and black pepper.

Note: If you use brown rice, cook the lentil and the rice together from the very beginning. You can also use bulgur instead of rice. This can be served with Armenian salad (page 18).

PIDEH
Cheese Beureg in Bread Dough

Filling:
1 egg
12 ounces white cheese, El Cacique
Queso Fesco (sold in Middle Eastern
markets), grated
4 ounces feta cheese, crumbled
½ cup fresh dill, chopped
½ teaspoon Aleppo red pepper
pinch of black pepper

1 pound ready-made bread dough

1. To make the filling, beat the egg in a bowl. Add the remaining filling ingredients and mix well.

2. Divide dough into 8 portions, form into balls and let rest for 5 minutes. Sprinkle flour on a board or counter top and with a rolling pin, roll each ball into 6-inch diameter rounds.

3. Divide the filling into 8 portions; place each along the diameter of each disk. Moisten (with water) the part of the edge of the dough that is within 1½ inches on either side of the edge of the filling. Using your fingers, squeeze together the moistened parts of the dough around each of the two edges of the filling. The resulting pideh should have dough covering the two edges where the filling is and an uncovered center where the filling is exposed.

4. Rest pideh for half an hour.

5. Preheat oven to 450 F degrees.

6. Bake pideh on a cookie sheet in the preheated oven for 12 minutes or until golden brown. Remove from oven and brush each one with melted butter. Serve warm.

PLAKI
White Bean Stew

1 cup cannellini beans, dry
⅓ cup extra virgin olive oil
2 Tablespoons tomato paste
1 medium tomato, chopped
1 green pepper, chopped
1 stalk celery and celery leaves, chopped
2 carrots, sliced diagonally
10 cloves peeled garlic, whole
1½ teaspoons salt
¼ teaspoon black pepper
1 teaspoon Aleppo red pepper
½ teaspoon sugar
½ cup cilantro, chopped
4 cups water
½ cup parsley leaves, chopped
1 Tablespoon lemon juice
2 Tablespoons extra virgin olive oil

1. Soak the beans overnight in water. Drain and rinse the beans. Place the beans in a pot and pour in fresh water to cover the beans. Bring the pot of beans to a boil over high heat, then turn off the heat and drain the beans.

2. Put the beans back in the pot, add remaining ingredients, except the parsley and lemon juice, then add the 4 cups of water and simmer covered for one hour or until the beans are very tender. Turn off the heat and add the parsley and lemon juice and mix. Drizzle with 2 tablespoons olive oil.

Serve at room temperature.

RADISH SALAD

10 radishes, grated
2 Tablespoons freshly squeezed lemon juice
1 Tablespoon extra virgin olive oil
salt to taste
Aleppo red pepper to taste

Mix all the ingredients together.

To serve, spread ½ inch flat layer on a plate and drizzle with olive oil and sprinkle with red pepper.

Note that larger radishes are easier to grate.

STRING BEANS WITH OLIVE OIL

¼ cup extra virgin olive oil
1 small onion, chopped
1 lb string beans, French cut (beans cut in half lengthwise)
6 cloves peeled garlic, whole
1 jalapeño pepper, diced, ¼ inch
½ red bell pepper, diced, ½ inch
6 medium tomatoes, diced, fresh or canned
1 teaspoon salt
¼ teaspoon black pepper
1 teaspoon sugar

1. In a pan, heat the oil and saute the onion until tender. Add the green beans and garlic, cover and simmer for 15 minutes, shaking the pan occasionally. Add the jalapeño and red bell peppers, tomatoes, salt, pepper and sugar.

2. Cover and simmer until tender, about 30 minutes. If the liquid has evaporated before the beans are tender, add some water and cook until beans are tender. If there is some liquid by the time beans are cooked, continue cooking until liquid evaporates. Serve cold or warm.

It is suggested to serve the beans with rice (page 80).

TABBOULEH
Lebanese Herb Salad with Bulgur

⅓ cup fine bulgur #1
½ cup lemon juice
3 medium ripe tomatoes, finely chopped
1 medium white onion, minced
¼ teaspoon allspice
3 bunches parsley, finely chopped
6 green onions, finely chopped
1 bunch fresh mint, finely chopped
1 teaspoon salt (or to taste)
½ teaspoon Aleppo red pepper
½ cup extra virgin olive oil
Romaine lettuce leaves

1. In a bowl, combine bulgur, lemon juice and chopped tomatoes. Let rest for 30 minutes so the bulgur softens.

2. Sprinkle the white onions with allspice and mix.

3. To the bowl with the softened bulgur, add the parsley, white onion mixture, green onions, mint, salt, red pepper, and olive oil. Toss with your hands and adjust seasonings.

You can eat the tabbouleh by itself or stuffed inside the inner leaves of romaine lettuce.

TAHNELI KUFTELI YAKHNI
Kufteh in Tahini Broth

Dough:
1½ cups fine bulgur #1
½ cup cream of wheat or semolina
¼ cup flour
dash of black pepper
½ teaspoon Aleppo red pepper
1 teaspoon salt
1 teaspoon cumin powder
1 small onion, finely chopped
½ cup water

Broth:
5 cups water
1 teaspoon salt
20 whole boiling onions, peeled
1 cup tahini
1 15 ounce can of garbanzo beans

lemon juice and Aleppo red pepper to taste

1. Knead bulgur, cream of wheat, flour, spices, and onion with ½ cup water in the food processor, until it becomes a lump.

2. Place in a bowl, take one teaspoonful of the dough, divide in 2 parts and roll them in the palm of your hand. They should be the size of small marbles. Process all the dough in this manner.

3. Boil 5 cups of water in a pot and add salt. As soon as the water boils, put the rolled kibbehs (marbles) in to cook for about 3 minutes. Take out the kibbehs from the water and set aside.

4. Add the peeled small onions to the water and cook for 5 minutes; remove them and put aside.

5. Temper the tahini paste with some of the broth and then put tempered tahini back into the pot and mix well. The sauce should be a little thick. Add the garbanzo beans, the kibbehs and the onions to the pot and stir.

Serve as a soup in a bowl and sprinkle with Aleppo red pepper, and squeeze lemon juice to taste.

VOSPOV KUFTEH
Kibbeh with Red Split Lentils

1 cup red split lentils
3 cups water
1 cup fine bulgur #1
1 teaspoon salt (or to taste)
1 teaspoon Aleppo red pepper
1 medium onion, chopped
½ cup olive oil
1 bunch parsley, chopped
1 bunch green onions, chopped

1. Wash and drain lentils, put them in a pot, add 3 cups water, bring to a boil. Simmer for 20 minutes or until lentil is very soft and there is little water left. Mix in the bulgur, salt, and red pepper. Cover and set aside for one hour or until it cools.

2. Sauté onions in the olive oil until translucent and set aside.

3. Place lentil mixture in a bowl, moisten your hands with warm water and knead for 2 minutes. Add the sautéed onions (with the oil) over the kneaded lentil mixture and continue kneading for one minute.

4. When it becomes one big lump, pinch off some of the mixture into walnut-sized pieces, squeeze each piece slightly in your lightly clenched fist and place on a serving plate. Shape all the mixture in this manner and plate. Sprinkle with chopped parsley and chopped green onions.

Note: Instead of pinching the lentil mixture one by one, you can spread it into a disk shape on a plate and sprinkle on the parsley and green onions.

YALANCHI SARMA
Stuffed Grape Leaves in Olive Oil

1 jar grape leaves
4 cups onions, finely chopped
1 cup long grain rice
½ cup extra virgin olive oil
1 Tablespoon tomato paste
½ cup currants or raisins
½ cup walnuts, chopped or pine nuts (or both)
½ bunch parsley, chopped
½ cup fresh mint leaves, chopped or 2 teaspoons dry mint
¼ cup fresh dill, minced or 1 teaspoon dry dill
1 Tablespoon sugar
6 Tablespoons lemon juice (4 Tablespoons in the filling and 2 in the liquid for cooking)
2 teaspoons salt
½ teaspoon black pepper
½ teaspoon Aleppo red pepper
½ teaspoon cinnamon
¼ teaspoon allspice
2 teaspoons lemon zest
3 cups water or enough to cover
1 lemon, cut into wedges

Preheat oven to 350 degrees F

1. Rinse the grape leaves in running hot water and remove the stems.

2. In a heavy skillet, sauté the onions on low heat (without oil) until translucent. Turn off heat. Rinse the rice and drain and stir into onions. Add the olive oil and the remaining ingredients except the water and mix well. This mixture (filling) should taste sweet and sour.

3. To stuff the grape leaves, place 1 Tablespoon of the filling along the stem end of each leaf (shiny side down), fold over the sides and roll from the stem up to form a wide and short roll.

4. Cover the bottom of the casserole with grape leaves, arrange the rolled grape leaves side by side, seam side down, layer by layer. Place a heavy plate over the top to keep the grape leaves in place while cooking.

5. Boil 3 cups of water with lemon juice and salt. Pour this on the stuffed grape leaves in the casserole and taste the liquid for salt and sourness.

6. Cover the casserole and bring it to a boil on top of the stove, then place in 350 F degrees preheated oven for one hour or until done. The rice should be very well-cooked.

7. Remove casserole from the oven and set aside to cool, covered.

8. Drain any remaining liquid into a bowl. Refrigerate the casserole with the stuffed grape leaves overnight. Remove the stuffed grape leaves (one by one so as not to damage them) and arrange on a serving plate. Garnish with lemon wedges.

MANAYISH
Bread with Thyme and Olive Oil

one package of frozen bread dough
12 Tablespoons zaatar (thyme and
sumac mixture sold in Middle Eastern
stores)
1-1/2 cups extra virgin olive oil (24
Tablespoons olive oil)

Preheat oven to 450 degrees F

1. Mix the zaatar with the olive oil and
put aside.

2. Defrost the dough, sprinkle flour
over your workspace, cut the dough
into 12 pieces and form each into a ball
(the size of a golf ball). Let rest for half
an hour.

3. Take one ball of dough, roll it with a
rolling pin to the size of a small pita
bread, spread one tablespoon of the
zaatar mixture on the dough. Do the
same with the rest of the balls of dough
and place them on a greased cookie
sheet. Let them rest for half an hour.
Bake them for 7 minutes in a preheated
oven at 450 degrees F.

Main
Dishes

MAIN DISHES

BAMIA
Okra Stew

1 lb beef shank or beef stew cut into 1 inch pieces
2 Tablespoons vegetable oil
1 small onion, chopped
4 cups water
1 15 oz can diced tomatoes
¼ cup lemon juice
¼ teaspoon allspice
¼ teaspoon black pepper
½ teaspoon Aleppo red pepper
1 teaspoon salt (to taste)
½ green bell pepper, chopped into ½-inch squares
1 lb okra, whole
1 clove garlic, minced
1 teaspoon cumin

1. Brown the meat in the oil with the onion, add the water and all the other ingredients, except okra, garlic and cumin. Bring to a boil, simmer covered for an hour or more, until meat is tender.

2. Remove stems from okra, wash. In a separate sauce pan, boil water with salt and 1 Tablespoon lemon juice, and blanch the okra. When tender, immediately strain and immerse the okra in ice water. When cool, drain and add to the stew. Cook until tender and add 1 teaspoon cumin and 1 clove minced garlic.

You can add cooked garbanzo beans to this stew.

Serve with rice pilaf (page 80).

BULGUR PILAF WITH MEAT OR CHICKEN

1 beef shank or 1 lb beef stew or 4
chicken thighs
6 cups water
2 bay leaves
whole black pepper and allspice corns
(3 corns of each)
1 teaspoon salt
¼ cup vermicelli cut into 1-inch
lengths
2 Tablespoons vegetable oil for frying
the vermicelli
1 small onion, chopped
1 Tablespoon butter
1 cup coarse bulgur #3 or #2
½ can (15 oz) garbanzo beans (optional)

1. Place meat or chicken thighs in a
pot. Add 6 cups of water, 2 bay leaves,
black pepper, allspice and salt. Bring to
a boil, remove the froth and simmer
covered for an hour and a half, until
meat is tender. Strain the broth and
degrease. Set aside the meat or
chicken thighs.

2. In a frying pan sauté vermicelli in
vegetable oil, remove with a slotted
spoon and set aside.

3. In the same pan, sauté lightly the
onions in butter. Add the bulgur and
continue to sauté. Add the garbanzo
beans, the sautéed vermicelli, 2¼ cups
of the broth and bring to a boil. Cover
and simmer for 20 minutes until all the
liquid is absorbed into the bulgur.

To serve, fluff the bulgur pilaf with a
fork, put in a serving platter, adding the
meat or chicken on top.

CHEUP KEBOB
Eggplant with Meat and Rice

1 lb ground beef, 15% fat
1 teaspoon salt
¼ teaspoon black pepper
¼ teaspoon allspice
1 teaspoon Aleppo red pepper
¼ cup breadcrumbs or oatmeal
2 Tablespoons milk
8 small Japanese eggplants (or Italian eggplants)
¼ cup vegetable oil
1 can (15 oz.) diced tomatoes
1 green bell pepper, sliced
salt to taste
1 teaspoon sugar

1. In a bowl, mix the ground beef with the salt and spices. Soak the bread crumbs or oatmeal in the milk and mix into the meat mixture. Divide into walnut sized meat balls.

2. Cut the eggplant crosswise into 2-inch pieces. Poke a toothpick lengthwise, halfway through each piece of eggplant. Add one meatball to each exposed toothpick anchoring them on the eggplant. Fry these eggplants formed with meat in vegetable oil and set aside. Also fry any left over meat balls.

3. In a saucepan, arrange the skewered eggplants and meat side by side.

4. Cover the eggplants and meat with the tomatoes (including liquid), and green peppers. Salt to taste and add 1 teaspoon sugar and simmer for half an hour.

Serve this with rice pilaf (page 80).

CHICKEN PILAF WITH ALMONDS AND CINNAMON

1 medium sized chicken (3 to 4 lbs)
2 bay leaves
6 peppercorns
1 slice lemon
4 Tablespoons butter
1 cup basmati or long grain rice
½ cup slivered almonds
1 Tablespoon cinnamon powder
1 teaspoon salt to taste

1. Place chicken in a pot, and cover with water, bring to a boil, skim the surface and discard. Add the bay leaves, 6 peppercorns and a slice of lemon. Bring to a boil, lower heat and cook for about one hour. Drain the broth in a strainer and degrease. Reserve the broth and let the chicken cool.

2. When chicken is cool, separate the meat from the bones in big chunks and set aside.

3. In a saucepan, melt the butter and add the cooked chicken pieces and sauté lightly. Rinse the rice and sauté by mixing it with the chicken pieces. Add 2 cups of broth to the rice and meat and bring to a boil, then simmer covered on very low heat until all the liquid is absorbed and rice is cooked. Remove from heat.

4. Toast the almonds and mix it into the chicken and rice along with the cinnamon. Fluff the rice and let rest for 20 minutes by covering it with a warm blanket or towel.

Serve with your favorite green salad.

EGGPLANT DOLMA
Eggplant Stuffed with Bulgur & Meat

You can serve this with Tahn (yogurt drink), watercress and white onions.

12 small Italian eggplants
2 tomatoes, whole
2 poblano or small green bell peppers, whole
2 red jalapeño or small red bell peppers, whole

Stuffing:
1 lb ground chuck
1 cup #4 bulgur
2 Tablespoons tomato paste
15 oz can diced tomatoes
2 Tablespoons finely chopped green peppers
2 teaspoons salt
1 teaspoon Aleppo red pepper
¼ teaspoon black pepper
1 teaspoon sumac powder
Tomato pulp

Cooking liquid:
2 cups water
4 Tablespoons sumac powder
½ teaspoon salt
3 Tablespoons vegetable oil

Tahn (yogurt drink):
1 cup yogurt
1 cup water
pinch of salt

1. Cut the eggplant one inch from the stem end, scoop out as much pulp as you can without puncturing the eggplant, with a vegetable corer or a thin long knife. Wash eggplants both inside and out and set aside.

2. Cut tomatoes quarter inch from the stem end. Using a teaspoon, scoop out the pulp of the tomatoes and reserve (to use in the stuffing). Keep the stem end to use as a cover after you stuff it. Cut the peppers a quarter inch from the stem end. Using a spoon or a thin knife, scoop out the seeds and ribs and discard.

3. Mix all the stuffing ingredients. Taste and adjust seasoning.

4. In a saucepan, add cooking liquid ingredients. Boil for 3 minutes, taste for sourness, add more sumac if it is not sour. Strain and add 3 Tablespoons vegetable oil and set aside.

5. Stuff the vegetables loosely leaving ½ inch empty space at the stem end. Arrange in a pot side by side, closely, first the eggplants, then the peppers, then the tomatoes on top. Pour the cooking liquid over the vegetables. The liquid should almost cover them (about ½ inch or less).

6. Place a plate, bottom side up, over the stuffed vegetables to hold them in place. Cover the pot, bring to a boil. Taste the liquid for salt and sourness and adjust as needed by adding sumac. The liquid should taste sour. Simmer until bulgur is cooked, about 30-40 minutes. Drain cooking liquid into a bowl (tilt the pot over a bowl while holding the vegetables in place with the inverted plate). Let stand for 5 minutes and serve. Drizzle a small amount of the cooking liquid on top of the dolmas.

7. To make the tahn, mix all the ingredients with a whisk and serve.

Note: You can replace bulgur with rice.

ZUCCHINI DOLMA
Zucchini Stuffed with Rice

Vegetables to be stuffed:
14 small zucchinis
3 tomatoes
2 green Anaheim peppers
1 red bell pepper

Stuffing:
1 lb ground chuck
1 cup long grain rice
15 oz can of tomatoes or 3 tomatoes, finely chopped
1 Tablespoon tomato paste
1 teaspoon Aleppo red pepper
¼ teaspoon black pepper
2 Tablespoons lemon juice
2 teaspoons salt

Cooking liquid:
2 cups water
¼ cup lemon juice
1 large clove garlic, crushed coarsely
1 Tablespoon crushed dry mint
1 teaspoon salt (to taste)
3 Tablespoons vegetable oil

1. Cut zucchinis 1 inch from the stem end. Scoop out pulp with a vegetable corer or a thin, long knife, leaving the walls of the zucchini about ⅓ inch thick. Wash zucchinis inside and out; set aside.

2. Cut the tomatoes a quarter inch from the stem end. Using a teaspoon, scoop out the pulp of the tomatoes and reserve (to use in the stuffing). Keep the stem end to cover tomato after stuffing. Cut the peppers a quarter inch from the stem end. Using a spoon or a thin knife, scoop out the seeds and ribs and discard.

3. Using your hands, thoroughly mix the stuffing ingredients and stuff vegetables loosely leaving 1 inch of empty space at the stem end.

4. In a small bowl, mix together cooking liquid ingredients; set aside.

5. Arrange all the stuffed vegetables in the pot side by side. If there is no space left, place the stuffed tomatoes on top. Pour the cooking liquid over the stuffed vegetables and cover with a plate (bottom side up). Bring to a boil, then cover and simmer for 30 minutes or until rice and vegetables are cooked. Drain cooking liquid into a bowl (tilt the pot over a bowl while holding the vegetables in place with the inverted plate). Cover the pot and let rest for 15 minutes, then serve. Make sure you drizzle some of the cooking liquid on top of the plate.

Serve with watercress, scallions or white onions.

FAKHDEH STAMBOULIEH
Meat Stew Topped with Yogurt

This is another dish with an unusual coupling of tastes and textures – meat and yogurt. The yogurt tames the spicy meat and sauce with such finesse that once you taste it you'll never forget the experience.

1 lb chuck roast
2 Tablespoons vegetable oil
1 small onion, coarsely chopped
1 small can tomato sauce
1 teaspoon salt
¼ teaspoon black pepper
¼ teaspoon allspice
¼ teaspoon Aleppo red pepper
2 bay leaves
3 cups warm water
pita bread, whole

Yogurt Sauce:
1 cup yogurt, strained
1 clove garlic, crushed
¼ teaspoon salt

1. Wash and cut meat into 2-3 inch chunks.

2. Sauté the meat and onions in 2 Tablespoons oil. Add the tomato sauce, spices, bay leaves and warm water. Cook covered until tender about 1 to 2 hours. The sauce should be reduced to a thick consistency. Stir the beef stew before serving.

3. In a bowl, mix the yogurt sauce ingredients.

4. Garnish individual stew servings with a dollop of the yogurt sauce. Serve with pita bread on the side.

FISH CASSEROLE
Aleppo Style

3-4 lbs of firm white fish for baking,
Whole (bone and head on) or fillet

Sauce:
1 large onion, thinly sliced
¼ cup extra virgin olive oil
1 Tablespoon tomato paste
1 Tablespoon red pepper paste
5 cloves of garlic, lightly crushed
½ bunch parsley or cilantro (or both),
chopped
½ cup red wine vinegar
2 cups water
salt to taste
¼ teaspoon black pepper
2 teaspoons cumin powder
2 teaspoons crushed coriander
one lemon, sliced
4 russet potatoes
vegetable oil

Preheat oven to 400 degrees F.

1. In a large frying pan, sauté sliced onion in olive oil until they are wilted. Add tomato paste, red pepper paste and continue to sauté. Add crushed garlic, chopped parsley (or cilantro), vinegar and water. Add salt, black pepper, cumin powder, coriander and lemon slices. Bring to a boil and set aside.

2. Peel and slice potatoes into ¼ inch circles. In a frying pan, heat the oil and fry the potatoes until lightly browned. Drain on paper towels. Salt them lightly.

3. Wash the fish inside and out, drain, then place in the middle of a big casserole dish. With a slotted spoon fill the cavity of the fish with a quarter of the sauce. Arrange the lightly fried potatoes around the fish.

4. Pour remaining sauce over the fish and potatoes. Bake at 400 F degrees for 30 to 45 minutes or until fish is flaky.

GREEN PEAS WITH MEAT

1 lb English short ribs
2 Tablespoons vegetable oil
Salt and black pepper to taste
1 Tablespoon tomato paste
3 cups water (or enough to cover meat)
2 carrots sliced diagonally
10 small pearl onions, peeled
1 lb fresh or frozen peas

1. Wash the meat and pat dry. In a large pot, heat the oil and brown the meat. Add salt, pepper, tomato paste, water and bring to a boil. Cover and simmer until meat is tender for about 2 hours.

2. Add the sliced carrots, peeled pearl onions and the fresh peas to the pot and cook for 15 minutes (if frozen peas are used, add them in the pot the last 5 minutes). Stew liquid should be thick when done.

Serve with plain rice (page 80).

HERISSA
Meat or Chicken with Hulled Barley

1 cup hulled barley (peeled wheat)
1 lb beef chuck or chicken, cut into 1 inch pieces
5 cups water (or enough to cover meat)
2 teaspoons salt
¼ teaspoon black pepper
2 bay leaves
¼ cup melted butter
1 teaspoon Aleppo red pepper
½ teaspoon cumin powder

1. Soak the barley overnight, drain.

2. In a large pot, add the meat and water and bring to a boil. Remove the froth with a spoon.

3. Add the barley, salt, black pepper and bay leaves to the pot and bring to a boil. Cover and simmer for 2 to 3 hours until the meat and barley are falling apart. It is preferable to use a slow cooker. With a wooden spoon mix the meat and the barley in the pot until it becomes a grainy purée.

4. In a small frying pan, melt the butter. Stir in the Aleppo red pepper and the cumin.

To serve, put 4 Tablespoons of the Herissa on a plate and drizzle with the prepared butter sauce.

KABOB KARAZ
Kabob with Cherries

The name literally means kabob with cherries, an unusual coupling of meat and sweet fruit, along the same vein as turkey and cranberries. The sweet and tart flavors of the cherries will taste foreign at first, but after a few mouthfuls you'll want more.

Kabob:
1 lb ground chuck
1 teaspoon salt
¼ teaspoon cinnamon
¼ teaspoon allspice
¼ teaspoon black pepper
½ teaspoon Aleppo red pepper
1 teaspoon baking soda
3 Tablespoons vegetable oil for frying the meatballs
2 Tablespoons pine nuts

Sauce:
24 oz. jar of pitted sour cherries in light syrup (sold in Middle Eastern markets) or fresh red cherries pitted
½ cup black or sour cherry jam
2 Tablespoons lemon juice
½ teaspoon Aleppo red pepper
¼ teaspoon allspice
¼ teaspoon black pepper
¼ teaspoon cinnamon
¼ teaspoon salt

1. Lightly mix all of the kabob ingredients, except the vegetable oil and the pine nuts. Taste and adjust the seasoning if necessary.

2. Roll the meat into 45 small marble-sized meatballs.

3. In a large frying pan heat the oil. Add the meatballs and fry 3-4 minutes until cooked. Remove them with a slotted spoon and set aside.

4. In a large saucepan add sauce ingredients. Mix together and bring to a boil. Taste and adjust seasoning (taste should be sweet and sour). Add the meatballs, bring to a boil and simmer for 10 minutes.

5. Separate 3 pita breads and cut into triangular pieces and lightly toast in oven. Arrange the bread on a serving platter in one layer.

6. Toast pine nuts in a pan with a little vegetable oil.

7. Pour the cherry sauce with the meatballs over the bread. Garnish with toasted pine nuts. Serve hot.

KIBBEH AL SIKH
Kibbeh on a Skewer

½ cup fine bulgur #1
⅓ cup water
1 lb ground beef (15% fat)
1 teaspoon salt (or to taste)
¼ teaspoon black pepper
½ teaspoon Aleppo red pepper
1 Tablespoon crushed dry mint
½ cup water (for processing the kibbeh)
1 Tablespoon onion, finely chopped
1 clove garlic, crushed
¼ cup extra virgin olive oil (for dipping the individual kibbehs in)

Preheat oven to 400 degrees F.

1. Soak the bulgur with ⅓ cup water in a food processor. After 15 minutes, add the meat and the rest of the ingredients except the olive oil and process until formed into a ball.

2. Put above mixture into a big bowl, divide dough into walnut-sized balls, shape each one on a skewer like a small hot dog about 2 inches long. Remove meat from the skewer, dip in the olive oil on all sides and arrange on a baking tray. Bake at 400 F degrees for 15 minutes, turn the tray as well as the Kibbehs so all sides bake evenly. Bake for another 10 minutes until golden brown.

3. Transfer baked kibbeh and oil from tray and place in a pot and sprinkle with water. Cover and put the pot on very low heat over the range for 10 minutes, shaking them occasionally. Pay attention not to burn.

Serve hot with cucumber Jajek (page 37) or a salad.

Note: It is better to grill this kibbeh instead of baking in the oven. There is no need to roll it in the olive oil if grilled.

KIBBEH MESHWIYEH
Grilled Kibbeh Balls

Kibbeh dough:
1¾ cups fine bulgur #1
½ cup cold water (for soaking the bulgur)
1 lb extra lean ground beef
2 teaspoons salt (or to taste)
1 teaspoon Aleppo red pepper
¼ teaspoon black pepper
1 Tablespoon onion, finely chopped
1 Tablespoon crushed dry mint
1 teaspoon cumin powder
½ cup cold water (for processing the kibbeh dough)

Filling:
1 stick unsalted butter
¼ teaspoon dried mint
¼ teaspoon black pepper
¼ teaspoon salt
¼ teaspoon crushed red pepper

2 Tablespoons water
2 Tablespoons extra virgin olive oil

1. Soak the bulgur with ½ cup of water for 30 minutes in a food processor. Add remaining kibbeh dough ingredients and process for 3 minutes, adding ½ cup water gradually until a medium-stiff dough ball forms. Transfer the mixture into a big bowl and knead with your hands until the mixture is smooth. Form into a ball and set aside.

2. Cut butter into ½ inch squares, sprinkle on crushed dry mint, black pepper, salt, and crushed red pepper. Refrigerate.

3. Cut dough into small walnut-sized balls. Make a deep hole in each (as described in Kufteli Yakhni) and stuff with one piece of the butter filling. After sealing the ball and rolling them in your palms, flatten the top and the bottom of the kibbehs by pressing them lightly between your palm and finger. Arrange them on a platter.

4. Grill the kibbehs on both sides on medium hot coals. Remove from the grill and place them in a pot, sprinkle on 2 Tablespoons water, add 2 Tablespoons olive oil and cover. Cover and simmer for 10 minutes on low heat, shaking occasionally. Serve hot with cucumber jajik (page 37) or a green salad.

KIBBEH NAYEH OR CHIY KUFTEH
Kibbeh with Raw Meat

1 lb Top of Round steak, cut into cubes and process in food processor into a paste; or kibbeh meat available at most Middle Eastern stores.
1½ teaspoons salt (or to taste)
⅛ teaspoon black pepper
1 cup bulgur #1
1 red bell pepper, chopped finely in the food processor
1 medium-sized onion, minced
2 teaspoons Aleppo red pepper
1 bunch parsley, chopped finely
4 stalks green onions, chopped finely
ice water in a small bowl

Salad for kibbeh nayeh:
2 tomatoes, chopped
½ cup parsley, chopped
½ onion, chopped
1 jalapeño pepper, chopped
½ cup green mint, chopped
1 Tablespoon lemon juice
2 Tablespoons extra virgin olive oil
½ teaspoon salt (or to taste)
1 teaspoon Aleppo red pepper

1. Process meat in the food processor with salt and black pepper for 3 to 4 minutes until it is like paste. Refrigerate.

2. In a mixing bowl, combine the bulgur with one finely chopped red bell pepper.

Mix well, then add in half of the minced onion and start kneading until well blended. Mix in half of the processed meat and the Aleppo red pepper. Knead while dipping your hands in the cold water periodically to keep your hands and the mixture moist. Once well mixed, add the remainder of the meat and knead an additional 2 minutes (continuing to dip your hands in cold water) until kibbeh is like a smooth dough. The consistency should be soft.

3. Moisten hands with cold water. Take a piece from the kibbeh mixture (as big as a tennis ball) and cut into small pieces the size of a walnut. Lightly squeeze each piece in the palm of your hand and place on a serving plate. Continue doing this by arranging one next to the other on the plate. Sprinkle with chopped parsley, chopped scallions and remainder of the chopped onion. Finally, sprinkle 1 to 2 Tablespoons cold water. An easier, but inferior, version of Kibbeh Nayeh can be made in a food processor. Simply put all the ingredients mentioned in step 2 in a food processor and process. After processing, spread it on a plate and cover with chopped onions and parsley and drizzle with olive oil.

4. Mix all salad ingredients and toss; serve alongside Kibbeh Nayeh.

KIBBEH SINIYEH
Kibbeh in a Tray

Kibbeh dough:
1¾ cups bulgur #1
½ cup cold water (for soaking the bulgur)
1 lb extra lean ground beef
2 teaspoons salt (or to taste)
1 teaspoon Aleppo red pepper
¼ teaspoon black pepper
1 Tablespoon onion, finely chopped
½ cup cold water (for processing the kibbeh)

Filling:
1 large onion, minced
1 Tablespoon butter, unsalted
¾ cup chopped walnuts
¼ cup pine nuts
½ teaspoon salt
⅛ teaspoon black pepper
¼ teaspoon Aleppo red pepper
⅛ teaspoon cinnamon
½ cup cold water (for forming the kibbeh dough over the filling)

3 Tablespoons extra virgin olive oil
2 Tablespoons water

Preheat oven to 300 degrees F

1. Soak the bulgur with ½ a cup of water for 30 minutes in a food processor. Add remaining kibbeh dough ingredients and process for 3 minutes, adding ½ cup water gradually until dough forms into a ball (it should be a medium-stiff dough).Put the kibbeh dough in a big bowl and, using your hands, form a big ball-(texture of the dough should be smooth). Set aside.

2. In a frying pan, lightly sauté onion in 1 Tablespoon butter. Add the walnuts and pine nuts and cook for 5 minutes. Remove from heat and mix in the salt, and all the spices. Set aside to cool. This can be prepared ahead.

3. Spread half of the kibbeh dough in a buttered or oiled 9X11-inch rectangular baking tray, pressing the kibbeh with the palm of your hands to form a smooth layer.

4. Spread the filling over the kibbeh. Flatten small portions (as big as tennis balls) of the remaining kibbeh dough between your hands and place them over the filling. Cover the entire surface of the filling in the tray with the kibbeh dough balls which have been flattened. Dip your hands in cold water and press down to even and smooth the surface (making sure the the surface is completely covered).

5. Pass a wet knife around the edges of the tray and cut the formed kibbeh into 2-in. diamond shapes or squares. Dot the surface with small pieces of butter, drizzle 3 Tablespoons of olive oil and sprinkle 2 Tablespoons water. Bake at 350 degrees F about 35-40 minutes or until lightly browned and top is firm.

KIBBEH TARABLOUSIEH
Stuffed Kibbehs with Ground Meat

Kibbeh dough:
1¾ cups bulgur #1
½ cup cold water (for soaking the bulgur)
1 lb extra lean ground beef
2 teaspoons salt (or to taste)
1 teaspoon Aleppo red pepper
¼ teaspoon black pepper
1 Tablespoon finely chopped onion
½ cup cold water (for processing the kibbeh)

Filling:
1 lb ground meat (15% fat)
1 large onion, minced
1 Tablespoon butter
¼ cup pine nuts
½ cup chopped walnuts
¼ teaspoon allspice
¼ teaspoon black pepper
½ teaspoon Aleppo red pepper
¼ teaspoon cinnamon
1 teaspoon salt
extra virgin olive oil (for coating kibbeh before baking)

3 Tablespoons extra virgin olive oil
2 Tablespoons water

Preheat oven to 350 degrees F

1. Prepare dough as in Kibbeh Siniyeh (kibbeh in the tray, page 72)

2. In a large frying pan, lightly saute onion in 1 Tablespoon butter. Crumble the ground meat and add to the onions. Cook on medium heat for 5 minutes, stirring occasionally. Add the walnuts and pine nuts and cook an additional 5 minutes. Remove from heat.

Mix in salt and spices. Set aside to cool. This can be prepared ahead.

3. Cut half of the kibbeh dough into egg-sized balls and roll between the palms of your hand to smooth the surface. Refrigerate the remainder of the dough covering with plastic wrap.

4. Hold a ball in your hand, push forefinger of your other hand inside the ball to make a hole. Press against the sides (all around) enlarging the hole. Fill the hole with one heaping teaspoon of the filling. Bring the edges of the opening together and seal. Roll the kibbeh between your palms until the kibbeh is smooth and oval-shaped, like a football. Shape all the balls in this manner. Take the remaining kibbeh dough from the refrigerator and knead it, dipping your hands in cold water until it is soft enough to form into balls. Repeat as above.

5. Put some olive oil in a small bowl. Dip each kibbeh in oil and arrange on a tray. Bake in 350 degree F oven for 20 minutes, until lightly browned. Take the tray out of the oven, turn the kibbeh over and bake another 10 minutes. Let cool. The cooked kibbeh can be refrigerated or frozen for later use.

6. To serve, place kibbeh in a pot and add 2 Tablespoons of Olive Oil. Sprinkle on 2 Tablespoons of water, cover and put on very low heat over the range for 15 minutes, shaking the pan frequently.

Note: Instead of baking, you can also lightly fry kibbehs in vegetable oil.

KUFTELI YAKHNI
Kibbeh in Yogurt Soup

This is a dish that is best served alone. Anything else served with it will be overshadowed. Add Aleppo red pepper before you dive into it to kick it up a notch.

Chicken Stock:
1 whole chicken (3-4 lbs.) or cut up chicken pieces
8 cups water
2 bay leaves
½ medium onion
1 lemon slice
1 piece fresh ginger, 2 inch section
1 teaspoon salt
¼ teaspoon ground black pepper

Filling:
¾ Stick (6 Tbsp,) unsalted butter (cubed into 60 pieces)
¼ teaspoon salt
¼ teaspoon black pepper or allspice

Kibbeh Dough:
1 lb. very lean ground beef or ready made meat for kibbeh (available in Middle Eastern stores)
1 Tablespoon grated onion
2 teaspoon salt
1 teaspoon Aleppo red pepper
1 cup cold water
1½ cup bulgur #1
¼ cup semolina or cream of wheat

Yogurt Mixture:
32 oz. yogurt
2 whole eggs
1½ cup chicken stock

Butter Topping:
2 Tablespoons butter
2 Tablespoons dry crushed mint

Chicken Stock:
1. In a large pot place the washed 3 lbs. whole chicken (or chicken pieces), add 8 cups water to cover and bring to a boil on high heat. Remove the scum which gathers on the surface with a spoon. Add remaining stock ingredients. Cover and cook on low medium heat for about an hour or until chicken is tender. Remove the chicken and set aside. Strain and degrease the stock and pour it back into the pot. Note: this dish tastes best when prepared with a stock made of a turkey carcass.

Filling:
1. Cut unsalted butter into ¼ inch cubes, sprinkle with salt and black pepper or allspice and refrigerate. Prepare this before you start making the kibbeh dough.

Kibbeh Dough:
1. Place the meat, onions, salt, red pepper and water (2 Tbsp.) in a food processor. Process for 1 minute.

2. Add the bulgur and semolina to the meat mixture in the food processor and process for 3 minutes, gradually adding 1 cup water. At this point the kibbeh dough should be well blended like a medium stiff dough.

3. Place the kibbeh dough in a big bowl and form it into a big lump, take one handful of kibbeh dough and pinch off pieces of kibbeh (the size of half a walnut) and shape into balls. Take one ball in your hand and make a hole, enlarging it to a size that is slightly bigger than the butter filling (to make the hole, hold a ball in the left hand, push forefinger of right hand inside the ball and press all around the wall, turning the ball around while pressing). Put one piece of seasoned butter filling in the hole, bring edges of opening together and seal. Roll the ball between palms to smooth the outside surface. Continue making balls until all the kibbeh dough has been used. While doing this, occasionally dip your hands in cold water. You should end up with about 60 kibbeh balls.

Cooking Instructions:
1. Bring the chicken stock to a boil, drop in half of the kibbeh balls and bring it back to a boil. Boil the kibbeh for 3 min. uncovered. Remove the balls from the pot and add the remaining uncooked balls. Repeat same procedure. Return the first batch of balls back to the pot. (After the 3 minute boil, they can be cooled, frozen and stored up to 4 months.)

2. Place yogurt and eggs in a bowl and whisk until smooth. Temper the yogurt by whisking in 1/2 cup of the hot stock to the yogurt. Whisk in an additional 1 cup hot stock. Pour the warm yogurt mixture into the pot, stirring constantly until it is very smooth. Bring this stock to a boil. Turn off heat.

3. Heat 2 Tbsp. butter in a small skillet until bubbly, add 2 Tbsp. crushed dry mint, stir and pour into the pot. Serve hot.

MANTI
Meat Dumplings in Yogurt Sauce

Dough:
1 package wonton wrappers, 9 x 9 inch sheets

Filling:
1 lb. ground chuck
1 small onion, minced
½ teaspoon salt
¼ teaspoon black pepper

Broth:
3 cups plain yogurt
1 egg
1 medium clove garlic, pressed
1 cup chicken broth
2 Tablespoons butter
1 Tablespoon crushed dry mint

Preheat oven to 350 degrees F

1. Lightly mix all the filling ingredients in a bowl and set aside.

2. Cut wonton dough horizontally and vertically into thirds forming 9 small squares. Place ½ teaspoon of the filling in the center of each square. Pinch the 2 ends together with your fingers to shape into a canoe shaped manti. Arrange with meat side up in a well-buttered 9X11 casserole dish and bake at 350 degrees F until golden brown (about 20-25 minutes).

3. Heat chicken broth in a small saucepan and set aside. In another saucepan, mix the yogurt with the egg and crushed garlic until smooth. Add salt to taste and heat it slightly. Temper the yogurt with one cup of hot chicken broth and heat on low to prevent curdling. When very warm pour over the manti.

4. Melt the butter and when bubbly add mint. Pour over the manti in the casserole dish. Serve immediately.

OURFA KABOB
Ground Meat and Eggplant Kabobs

Ourfa Kabob, the Aleppo version of this Turkish dish named after the city of Ourfa, is a traditional dish that contrasts the hearty flavor of the simply spiced meat with the delicate texture and subtle taste of eggplant. After cooking, sprinkle it lightly with salt and black pepper.

1 lb ground chuck
1 teaspoon baking soda
1 teaspoon salt (to taste)
1 teaspoon Aleppo red pepper
¼ teaspoon black pepper
¼ teaspoon allspice
8 Italian eggplants
bamboo skewers
2 Tablespoons water
2 Tablespoons butter
4 Roma tomatoes, whole
4 green peppers, whole (preferably Anaheim or poblano)

1. Soak bamboo skewers in water for 5 minutes.

2. Mix the ground meat with the baking soda and spices until well blended. Divide into walnut sized balls. Set aside.

3. Cut the eggplants crosswise into 2-inch circles the same size as the meatballs so they will cook evenly. Take a bamboo skewer and thread 5 eggplant pieces and 4 meatballs alternately. Continue doing this until you finish all the meatballs and the eggplant pieces. Grill these on a hot fire, approximately 10 minutes, turning occasionally until the meat is cooked and the eggplant is tender and the skin is slightly charred. Remove from the grill and arrange them in a 9X11 baking pan as you pull out the skewers. Drizzle two tablespoons of water and dot them with some butter. Cover with foil and leave on the grill on low heat for 30 minutes.

4. Serve with grilled tomatoes and green peppers.

RICE PILAF

1 cup basmati rice
1 Tablespoon salt (for soaking)
1½ cups hot water
1 Tablespoon butter
¼ teaspoon salt

1. Put uncooked rice in a small pot. Add 1 Tablespoon salt and cover with hot water. Let it soak for at least an hour. Rinse the rice thoroughly with cold water in a sieve and let it drain.

2. Melt butter in a pot and when hot, add 1½ cups of hot water, ¼ teaspoon salt and bring to a boil. Add the rinsed and drained rice, stir lightly, bring to a boil. Cover and simmer on very low heat, about 10 minutes, until all the water is absorbed. Don't open the lid of the pot while it is simmering. After 10 minutes remove the lid to see if the water has been absorbed and there are holes on the surface of the rice which means it is cooked. Remove from heat and wrap the pot with a towel and let it rest for about 15 minutes. Fluff the rice with a fork and serve.

Note: To make rice with Vermicelli, increase the water by ¼ cup. Cut 3 Tablespoons of vermicelli by hand into 1-inch pieces, fry in oil, take it out with a slotted spoon and add to the rice in the pot before it starts simmering.

SARMA
Stuffed Cabbage Leaves with Ground Meat & Rice

2 heads of cabbage
1 lb ground chuck
1 cup Basmati rice, rinsed
2 tomatoes, finely chopped
1 Tablespoon tomato paste
½ green bell pepper, finely chopped
2 teaspoons salt (or to taste)
½ teaspoon black pepper
¼ teaspoon allspice
½ teaspoon Aleppo red pepper

Cooking liquid:
3 teaspoons crushed dry mint
2 cups water
3 cloves of garlic, crushed coarsely
6 Tablespoons lemon juice
1 teaspoon salt
3 Tablespoons vegetable oil

1. Bring a large pot of water to boil.

2. Remove the entire core of the cabbage with a paring knife. Immerse the head of cabbage in the boiling water. Parboil until limp and cabbage leaves are easy to roll, about 5 minutes. Drain in a colander. Using tongs, carefully peel off each leaf. Slice each leaf in half along the rib section, discarding the ribs. Save one large cabbage leaf.

3. Combine ground chuck, washed rice, chopped tomatoes, tomato paste, chopped green pepper, salt, black pepper, all spice, red pepper and mix by hand.

4. Prepare cooking liquid by combining all the cooking liquid ingredients in a bowl.

5. Place 1 Tablespoon of the filling along the bottom of each leaf. Fold over the sides (you can do without folding the sides if you want) and roll. Cover the bottom of a large pot or Dutch oven with the (uncut) large cabbage leaf. Layer the cabbage rolls, seam side down, side by side in the pot until all cabbage rolls have been placed. Place a heavy plate over the rolled cabbages. Pour in the cooking liquid, cover and bring to a boil. Simmer for 40 minutes or until leaves are tender. Let rest for 10 minutes. Empty the liquid in the pot into a bowl. Remove the heavy plate and invert the contents of the pot on to a round serving platter.

Serve with yogurt, green onions and watercress on the side.

SARMA
Stuffed Grape Leaves with Meat & Rice

1 jar grape leaves (available in Middle Eastern markets)

Filling:
1 cup Basmati rice, rinsed
1 lb ground chuck
½ Tablespoon tomato paste
1 large tomato, finely chopped
1 Tablespoon lemon juice
2 teaspoons salt
¼ teaspoon ground all spice
¼ teaspoon black pepper
½ teaspoon Aleppo red pepper
1 head of garlic, divided into individual cloves and peeled
¼ cup vegetable oil

Cooking liquid:
2½ cups water
3 Tablespoons lemon juice
½ teaspoon salt (or to taste)

1. Wash the grape leaves and cut off the stems.

2. Mix all the filling ingredients (except the garlic). Take a grape leaf, (if very large cut in half) and place shiny side down on a flat surface. Place about ½ Tablespoon of the filling along the stem end of each leaf. Fold over the sides and roll from the stem up. Continue until all the leaves are done. Cover the bottom of a large pot with some grape leaves. Arrange the stuffed grape leaves, stem side down, side by side in the pot. Scatter a few peeled cloves of garlic. Continue layering stuffed grape leaves and garlic cloves into the pot. Place a heavy plate over the top to keep stuffed grape leaves in place while cooking.

3. Pour the cooking liquid over the stuffed grape leaves. Bring to a boil, and reduce heat and cook for 30 to 40 minutes, until tender. Let rest for 10 minutes then drain the broth into a bowl. Let rest for another 10 minutes, then invert contents of the pot on a round serving platter. Remove and discard the loose grape leaves. Serve with yogurt on the side.

SHEIKH EL MEHSHI
Stuffed Zucchini with Meat in Yogurt Sauce

This is a unique dish that incorporates a yogurt sauce sprinkled with pine nuts and gives the classic stuffed zucchini an entirely unusual and delicately flavored reincarnation. Served with rice, it is a true delicacy of Aleppo.

12 small zucchinis

Stuffing:
½ lb ground beef (15% fat)
1 egg
2 Tablespoons bread crumbs or corn flake crumbs
¼ cup parsley, minced
2 Tablespoons pine nuts, toasted
¼ teaspoon ground black pepper
¼ teaspoon ground allspice
small pinch of nutmeg
½ teaspoon salt
¼ cup vegetable oil (for frying)

Sauce:
2 cups yogurt, strained
1 egg

1. Cut off top of zucchini, scoop out pulp with a small melon baller (or tool sold at Middle Eastern stores). Wash zucchinis inside out and set aside.

2. Mix all the stuffing ingredients using your hands and stuff the zucchinis. If there is stuffing left over, make small meatballs.

3. Heat vegetable oil in a frying pan. Lightly fry the stuffed zucchinis (and the meat balls). Put the zucchini and the meatballs in a pot. Add 2 cups of water and bring to a boil. Cover and simmer for 15 minutes.

4. In a bowl, whisk the egg with the strained yogurt until smooth.

5. Temper the yogurt mixture with the hot liquid from the zucchini pot. Pour half the yogurt mixture into the zucchini pot and cook gently for another 15 minutes until the zucchinis are fork tender.

6. Add the remaining yogurt mixture and bring to a light boil. Adjust salt. The sauce should be thick, like a creamy soup.

Serve with rice pilaf (page 80).

SHWEIDIS
Leek Stew in Yogurt Sauce

3 large leeks
1 beef shank, cut into 2-inch chunks
5 cups water
1 teaspoon salt
2 bay leaves
1 (2 lbs) container of yogurt, strained
2 Tablespoons butter
1 Tablespoon crushed dry mint

1. Discard 2 inches off the green end of the leaks and remove stem end. Starting from the stem end, cut the leak crosswise toward the green end into 1 inch slices. Soak in water thoroughly rinsing and removing any soil. Drain and set aside.

2. Wash the meat and put in a pot. Add the water and bring to a boil. Remove froth off the top. Add the salt and bay leaves, cover and simmer for 2 hours or until meat is tender.

3. Drain and reserve broth through a sieve; there should be about 3 cups. Put the meat and the broth back into the clean pot. Add the leaks and bring to a boil. Cover and simmer about 15 minutes or until leak is tender.

4. Place the yogurt in a bowl, add one egg and beat with a whisk until very smooth. Add a little of the hot broth into yogurt mixture to temper it. Continue adding more broth in this manner until it is lukewarm. Pour the yogurt mixture into the pot and stir constantly until it comes to a boil. Turn off the heat and add salt to taste.

5. In a small frying pan, melt 2 Tablespoons butter and add the crushed mint. As soon as it sizzles, pour into the pot. Let it rest for 15 minutes so the yogurt sauce thickens (it should be thick like a cream soup).

Serve with rice pilaf with vermicelli (page 80)

STEWED FRESH FAVA BEANS

This is a simple dish based on humble ingredients yet the combination of fresh Fava beans (whose season runs from Spring to early Summer) with the yogurt sauce give it an exotic taste.

1 lb. fresh fava bean pods
1 beef shank cut into 2" pieces
1 small onion, chopped
1 Tablespoon tomato paste
6 cloves garlic, peeled
1 teaspoon Salt
½ teaspoon Aleppo red pepper
¼ teaspoon Black pepper
2 Tablespoons Vegetable oil
3 cups water

Yogurt sauce
2 cups yogurt
2 cloves garlic, minced
Salt to taste

Bulgur pilaf
1 cup bulgur No. 2 or 3
2 ¼ cups water
2 Tablespoons Butter
½ teaspoon salt

1. Trim off the edges of each pod of fava bean and pull off the string that runs across the length of the pod. Cut the pods into 2" pieces.

2. Put the vegetable oil in a pot and brown the shank pieces and the shank bone. Add the salt, black pepper and Aleppo red pepper. Next add the onions and sauté for a few minutes. Add the tomato paste and mix well. Add the water, bring to a boil, lower heat, cover and simmer for about an hour and a half or until meat is tender. Add water if contents of the pot get dry. Once the meat is tender add the fava bean pods, add some salt to taste (1/2 tsp.) and cook until they are tender, about 20-25 minutes.

Yogurt sauce:
To make yogurt sauce, mix the yogurt with the minced garlic and add salt to taste.

Bulgur Pilaf:
To cook bulgur pilaf, in a pan sauté bulgur in 2 Tbsp. butter for a few minutes, add the water, 1/2 tsp. Salt and bring to a boil, then cover and simmer on very low heat for about 30-35 minutes until bulgur is soft.

Serve the stewed fava bean pods drizzled with some yogurt sauce along side. Serve with rice pilaf (page 80.

STRING BEANS WITH MEAT

1 lb string beans
1 Tablespoon butter
½ lb ground beef (15% fat) or 1 beef shank cut in 2-inch chunks
1 small onion, chopped
½ green bell pepper, sliced
½ red bell pepper, sliced
1 lb can of plum tomatoes, chopped
6 cloves of garlic
1 teaspoon salt (or to taste)
½ teaspoon Aleppo red pepper
¼ teaspoon black pepper

1. Wash the string beans, trim them and slice lengthwise.

2. In a frying pan, melt the butter and sauté the onions over medium heat. Add the ground beef and continue cooking for 5 minutes. Add the string beans, green and red bell peppers, garlic, salt, and sauté for about 10 minutes. Add the tomatoes, cover and cook on low heat for about an hour or until the string beans are tender.

Note: When using shank, wash the shank, pat dry and sauté in 2 Tablespoons of oil until browned. Add the salt and pepper, the onions, chopped tomatoes (with the juice which is in the can). Cover and cook on medium low heat until meat is almost cooked. Add the string beans with the garlic and green and red bell peppers and cook until meat and vegetables are tender. While cooking, pay attention to the juice in the pan. If needed, add some water to avoid burning.

Serve with rice pilaf (page 80) and jajek (page 37).

WHITE BEANS WITH MEAT
Armenian Cassoulet

1 lb beef shank cut into 2-inch chunks
2 Tablespoons butter
1 cup cannellini or great northern beans
1 Tablespoon tomato paste
1 teaspoon salt
¼ teaspoon black pepper
½ teaspoon Aleppo red pepper
1 small onion, chopped
1 clove garlic
2 bay leaves
4 cups water

1. Soak white beans in cold water overnight. For quick soaking, put beans in a pot with some cold water, bring it to a boil and turn off heat. Let stand for 2 hours, drain beans.

2. In a large pot, melt the butter and brown the shank meat and the bone on all sides. Add the onions and sauté for five minutes. Add salt, pepper, crushed red pepper, tomato paste, garlic, 4 cups water, 2 bay leaves, and beans and bring to a boil. Cover and simmer. Cook until very tender about two hours. Discard the bay leaves.

Serve with rice pilaf (page 80).

Desserts

DESSERTS

• • •

BHAKLAVA

Filling:
2 cups walnuts, chopped
1 teaspoon cinnamon
3 Tablespoons sugar

Syrup:
1 cup sugar
½ cup water
1 teaspoon lemon juice
1 Tablespoon orange blossom water

1 package of Philo pastry sheets
1 cup melted butter

Preheat oven to 350 degrees F.

1. Mix all the filling ingredients in a bowl.

2. In a sauce pan, combine water, sugar and lemon juice and bring to a boil. Continue boiling for 2 minutes. Add orange blossom water, turn off heat and set aside. Cool before use.

3. Butter a 9x13 pan. Unroll the philo pastry sheets on your work table. Place 2 philo sheets in the pan, folding the sheets as necessary to fit the pan. Brush the surface of the sheet with the melted butter. Repeat this process 3 more times (for a total of 8 sheets). Spread the filling mixture on the surface. Add 8 more sheets using the same method as the first 8 Philo sheets.

4. With a wet serrated knife, cut the philo sheets into approximately 2 inch squares. Bake until the surface is golden brown, approximately 30 minutes. Remove from oven and pour the cool syrup all over the surface. For a puffier and richer Baklava, boil ½ cup of butter and pour it on the surface of the pan as soon as you remove it from the oven.

BAKLAWA FRANJIEH
Aleppo Dessert with Semolina

3 Tablespoons unsalted butter
6 cups milk
2 Tablespoons sugar
1 cup yellow semolina
2 Tablespoons orange blossom water
¼ cup powdered sugar
cinnamon

Preheat oven to 450 degrees F.

1. Grease a 10 x 13-inch baking pan with 3 Tbsp of butter and set aside.

2. Pour the milk into a saucepan, add the 2 Tbsp. of sugar and bring to a boil over high heat. Add semolina and cook on low heat stirring continuously with a whisk for a few minutes, until the

mixture thickens. Mix in orange blossom water. Remove from heat.

3. Pour the mixture into the greased baking pan and tap the pan a few times to eliminate the air bubbles. Let it cool then place in the refrigerator for 3 hours or overnight. Using a knife that has been dipped in water, cut the Baklawa Franjieh into 2 inch squares.

4. Bake for approximately 35 minutes or until golden brown.

5. To serve, using a spatula remove the squares from the pan. Sprinkle each serving with powdered sugar and cinnamon.

HADIG
Boiled Whole Wheat with Spices, Sugar and Nuts

1 cup whole wheat grains, rinsed and drained
3 cups water
½ teaspoon anise seed
½ teaspoon fennel seed
½ cup cooked garbanzo beans (rinsed and drained)
2 teaspoons cinnamon
sugar to taste
1 cup walnut, coarsely chopped and toasted
1 Tablespoon sugar-coated anise candies
½ cup pomegranate seeds

1. Soak wheat in cold water overnight. Place rinsed and drained whole wheat grains in a pot, add 3 cups water, add anise and fennel seeds and bring to a boil. Simmer uncovered for about 2 hours until wheat grains are soft and all the water is absorbed. Add garbanzo beans and mix.

2. Place the cooked wheat grains in a big bowl, mix in cinnamon and sugar and transfer to a platter. Cover with the walnuts, sugar-coated anise candies, and pomegranate seeds. Serve warm.

HAYTALIYEH
Milk Custard with Orange Blossom Water

This is a quintessential summer dessert. It is a true delight.

4 cups milk
1 package of gelatin
1 cup water
9 Tablespoons cornstarch
shaved or crushed ice
vanilla ice cream

Syrup:
1½ cups sugar
¾ cup water
2 Tablespoons orange blossom water
1 teaspoon lemon juice

1. In a small pot, pour the milk. Mix the gelatin into the milk and let stand for 5 minutes. Bring the milk to a boil. In a small bowl, mix the cornstarch with one cup of water until smooth, temper with the hot milk, then pour the dissolved cornstarch into the milk, stirring with a whisk continuously until it bubbles and the mixture has lightly thickened (about 2 minutes).

2. Pour the mixture into a 10 x 13-inch pan which has been sprinkled with water. Let it partially cool until it forms a thin skin on the surface. Prepare one cup of ice water and pour it into your palm and gently sprinkle over the mixture, trying not to break the skin. This is done to wrinkle the skin. After cooling, refrigerate overnight until it jells.

3. To make syrup, mix together water, sugar and lemon juice. Bring to a boil and let boil for 3 minutes, then add the orange blossom water and turn off heat.

4. To serve, cut the jelled cold mixture into 1-inch squares. With a spatula take out 4 squares or more and put in individual small serving bowls and add ¼ cup of the syrup on top of the squares, add 2 Tbsp shaved or crushed ice and top it with 1 scoop of vanilla ice cream. Sprinkle chopped pistachio nuts and serve.

KADAIF OR KUNEFEH
Shredded Wheat with Ricotta Cheese

Syrup:
1½ cups sugar
¾ cup water
1 teaspoon lemon juice
2 Tablespoons orange blossom water

1 pound package kadaif (shredded wheat)
1 cup (2 sticks) unsalted butter, melted

Cheese Filling:
15 oz. ricotta cheese, part skim

Preheat oven to 400 degrees F.

1. Prepare the syrup by combining the sugar and water in a saucepan. Bring to a boil over high heat. Reduce heat and add the lemon juice. Simmer about 5 minutes. Stir in the orange blossom water. (Note, you can judge the thickness after it gets cold. If it is too thick, add a few teaspoons of warm water. When cooled, the thickness should be less than that of honey.)

2. Place kadaif in a large bowl and shred with fingers, gradually adding the melted butter until all is evenly shredded and coated with butter.

3. Remove Ricotta cheese from container and cut into 1/2 inch slices.

4. Spread half of the shredded kadaif into an 8 x 12-inch baking pan and press. Place the ricotta cheese slices evenly over the whole surface. Now cover this surface with the remaining shredded kadaif, cover with wax paper or aluminum foil and press the surface down firmly.

5. Add a weight, for example a small cutting board, on the second layer of shredded wheat and let it sit for half an hour.

6. Remove the weight, foil or wax paper and bake for 30 minutes or until kadaif has a nice, golden color. Let it cool for 10 minutes then cut into 2½-inch squares. Pour half of the cooled syrup over the kadaif. Serve the remaining syrup in a sauce bowl on the side.

KARABIJ
Walnut Stuffed Pastry with Marshmallow Topping

Dough:
2 cups unsalted butter (4 sticks)
1 Tablespoon Crisco
¾ cup plus 2 Tablespoon water
4 cups cream of wheat
1 cup of semolina
2 teaspoons mahlab (sold in Middle Eastern stores)

Filling:
2 cups chopped walnuts (in a food processor pulse walnuts about 10 pulses or until they are just bigger than lentils)
3 Tablespoons sugar
2 teaspoons cinnamon
2 Tablespoons orange blossom water

1 jar marshmallow topping

Preheat oven to 325 degrees F

1. Put the butter, the Crisco, and the water in a small pot and heat until butter melts.

2. In a bowl, mix the cream of wheat and semolina with the mahlab, then pour in the butter mixture and mix well until wet. Keep covered overnight or at least 2 hours. Knead the cream of wheat mixture in the bowl until it looks like a pie dough and is malleable. Shape into walnut-sized balls (this will make about 60 balls).

3. Prepare filling: mix all ingredients together and set aside.

4. With a ball in your left hand palm, press an opening with your right forefinger. Continue to turn the ball in your left hand palm while gradually enlarging the opening in the ball with your forefinger, pressing against the sides of the ball. Fill cavity with one heaping teaspoon of the walnut filling. Carefully seal the opening, creating an oval shape like a football and smooth it gently with your fingers.

5. Repeat this process with the rest of the balls and arrange them on a cookie sheet. Refrigerate for 3 hours or overnight.

6. Bake in a 325 degree F. oven on top shelf for 30 minutes. When you remove from oven it will be soft to the touch. Let it cool completely. Refrigerate if not serving immediately.

7. To serve, bring karabij to room temperature, top each one with 1 teaspoon of marshmallow topping and sprinkle with powdered cinnamon.

Note: Spray the teaspoon with Pam so marshmallow will slide easily from the spoon onto the karabij.

KOURAYBIA
French Style Shortbread

½ lb unsalted butter (2 sticks), softened
1 egg yolk
¼ cup vegetable oil
2 Tablespoons lemon juice
½ teaspoon baking soda
1 cup powdered sugar
3 cups flour

Preheat oven to 300 degrees F.

1. Mash the butter, add egg yolk and mix. Add the vegetable oil, lemon juice, baking soda, ½ cup powdered sugar and mix. Using your hands, add flour gradually and form into a ball. Refrigerate for half an hour.

2. Cut dough into 4 parts. Roll out each part to about 1 inch thickness. Cut diagonally into 3 inch pieces. Line the pieces on a baking sheet and bake for 25 minutes. Remove from oven and let it cool in the tray. Sprinkle generously with the remaining powdered sugar.

This can be stored in a refrigerator up to one month.

MAMOUNIEH
Aleppo Breakfast Pudding

1 cup sugar
4 cups water
1 cup cream of wheat
½ cup unsalted butter (1 stick)
1 Tablespoon orange blossom water
1 pinch ground cinnamon
1 Tablespoon chopped unsalted raw pistachios

1. In a saucepan, bring the water and sugar to a boil.

2. In a frying pan, sauté the cream of wheat in butter until lightly golden.

3. Pour the sautéed cream of wheat into the boiled sugar water. Add the orange blossom water. Lightly stir, cover and take off the heat. Leave it to rest for 10 minutes, then transfer to a serving dish. Sprinkle with cinnamon and pistachios.

MBATTANEH

Traditional Christmas Rice Pudding. A must according to Noubar, Seta's husband and Rhoda's brother.

Rice Pudding:
⅓ cup short or medium grain rice
1 cup water
6 cups milk

Thickened Orange Juice:
2 cups orange juice
6 Tablespoons sugar, more if needed
2 teaspoons orange rind
2 Tablespoons cornstarch
2 Tablespoons water

½ cup blanched, peeled, and halved almonds or slivered almonds

1. Rinse rice, place into a pot and add 1 cup water and bring to a boil. Use a thick-bottomed pot. Cover and simmer until water is absorbed about 5 to 10 minutes. Add 6 cups of milk to the rice and bring to a boil. Turn down the heat and simmer 45-50 minutes uncovered, stirring frequently until rice is cooked and is creamy. If it is too thick, add some milk.

2. About 10 minutes before rice is cooked, prepare the thickened orange juice. In another pot, mix the orange juice, sugar and orange rind and bring to a boil. In a small bowl, mix cornstarch in 2 tablespoons water. Temper with a little hot orange juice and pour the dissolved cornstarch into the pot that contains the orange juice. Stir with a whisk until it is smooth.

Note: Have the rice pudding and the thickened orange juice ready at the same time.

3. Pour the thickened orange juice into small dessert bowls until half full (about 4 Tablespoons). Then spoon the rice pudding into the center of the thickened orange juice, until the bowl is almost full (about 4 tablespoons). Sprinkle with blanched, halved almonds or slivered almonds and let cool. The mbattaneh can be eaten warm or cold.

Index

CPSIA information can be obtained
at www.ICGtesting.com
Printed in the USA
BVHW02n0214120318
509872BV00003B/6/P